THE SKY BEHIND THE FOREST

Liliana Ursu, an already important Romanian poet, is now becoming increasingly well known internationally. She has written seven books of poetry. Born in 1949 in the city of Sibiu in the Carpathian mountains of Transylvania, she came of age in Bucharest during the debilitating years under Ceaucescu's crushing régime. In 1972 she graduated with a degree in English from the University of Bucharest, where she taught part-time for the rest of the decade. Her recent collection, *Port Angeles* (from which almost a quarter of the poems in this book are taken), has awaited publication for more than four years in Romania. Meanwhile she has continued to write and over a third of the poems in *The Sky Behind the Forest* are new poems, written since the Port Angeles volume reached the Romanian publisher in spring of 1992. Many of them appear in her latest volume, *Angel Riding the Beast*, published in Bucharest in December 1996. Her first book, *Life Above the City*, was published in 1977. Lilana Ursu's other poetry titles include *Time Sequences* (1978), *The Goldsmiths' Market* (1980), *Safety Zone* (1983), and *Coral* (1987). She has won three Romanian literary prizes for her poems.

Liliana Ursu has also published two books of short stories and six books of translation, which include the work of American, British, and Flemish poets into Romanian, and that of Romanian writers into English. She lives in Bucharest, where, since 1980, she has had an acclaimed weekly literary programme on Romanian Radio which features interviews, poetry, and book reviews, with a special focus on contemporary world poetry. In 1992-93 she was a visiting professor at Pennsylvania State University on a Fulbright grant.

LILIANA URSU

The Sky Behind the Forest

SELECTED POEMS

translated by LILIANA URSU *with*
ADAM J SORKIN *and* TESS GALLAGHER

BLOODAXE BOOKS

ISBN: 1 85224 386 4

First published 1997 by
Bloodaxe Books Ltd,
P.O. Box 1SN,
Newcastle upon Tyne NE99 1SN.

Bloodaxe Books Ltd acknowledges
the financial assistance of Northern Arts.

Thanks are due to the Arts Council of England
for providing a translation grant for this book.

Cover printing by J. Thomson Colour Printers Ltd, Glasgow.

Printed in Great Britain by
Cromwell Press Ltd, Broughton Gifford, Melksham, Wiltshire.

for my parents, Elena and Ioan

ACKNOWLEDGEMENTS

Acknowledgements are due to the editors of the following publications in which some of these poems appeared, some in somewhat different English versions: *Fires on Water: 7 Poets from Sibiu*, edited by Adam J. Sorkin and Liliana Ursu (Bucharest: Editura Cartea Româneasca, 1992): 'Seascape', 'Poem for a Brother in Spirit', 'Bait', 'Double Portrait', 'Contre Jour', 'Title It as You Like', 'Anatomy of a December Night', and 'Port Angeles'; and have appeared or are forthcoming in the following periodicals: *Passages North*: 'Anatomy of a December Night', 'Bait', 'Seascape', 'You Haven't a Face', and 'Port Angeles'; *Visions International*: 'Contre Jour', 'Couple', 'With One Eye We Cry, with the Other We Laugh', 'Bison Hunting', 'Double Portrait', and 'Really, Don't You Believe Me?'; *Kalliope: A Journal of Women's Art*: 'Above the Bridge', 'Silent Voices', and 'Moment with Thunder'; *The Snail's Pace Review*: 'Season's End'; *Penn State Liberal Arts Review*: 'Poem for a Brother in Spirit'; *Delos: A Journal of Translation and International Literature*: 'Contrasts', 'For Constantin Noica', 'In the Dusk', 'Spring in Dream', 'The Mirror's Hide and Seek', and 'Is This Wisdom?'; *American Poetry Review*: 'In the Forest', 'Portrait with Dandelions', 'Dialogue', 'Humility', and 'Death in Spring'; *The New Yorker*: 'Rain in Sibiu', 'Life Under Ground', and 'In the City of What Once Was'; *Sycamore Review*: 'Poem for Tess', 'The Moon', 'Noroc', and 'Orpheus'; *Columbia*: 'Unforgetting', 'Evening after Evening', 'The Goldsmiths' Market', 'From the Angel's Window', 'Diana's Shadow', 'Blues', 'Spring Circumstance', and 'Ancient and Beautiful as the Mist'.

Liliana Ursu expresses thanks to the Fulbright Scholar Program and Penn State University for support during her year in America during which much work was accomplished toward this book. Adam Sorkin wishes to express appreciation to the Fulbright Scholar Program and the International Research and Exchanges Board (IREX), as well as to Penn State University for support of his work on these translations. Tess Gallagher is thankful to the Lyndhurst Foundation for support during the time she undertook these translations. This support also financed the extensive and painstaking typing and retyping of the manuscript through all its various stages. To Dorothy Catlett, who worked patiently and lovingly on the typescript as secretary to the project, and who kept communication flowing between Bucharest, Havertown and Port Angeles, we all give our heartfelt thanks. Henry Carlile, poet and friend, deserves kind thanks for going over the manuscript as it entered its final stage of readiness. Greg Simon, a translator of Federico García Lorca and poet in his own right, made helpful suggestions for which we are also thankful.

CONTENTS

INTRODUCTION

Many of us in Berkeley first heard the work of Liliana Ursu in April 1993 when she was unable to come here; upon the sudden death of her father during her Fulbright year in the U.S. she had been called back to Romania. While she ministered to her family in Bucharest, her newly translated poems were being read by Tess Gallagher in the packed, close, upstairs reading room of Cody's Bookstore, a room where the long strings that dangle from the ceiling fans sometimes collude with mythic forces and make splendid, pronounced haloes over the visiting poets. This was a little over three years after the overthrow of the terrible Ceaucescu government, the beginning of slightly more hopeful days for Romanian writers. Although Ceaucescu was gone, the reflexes and effects of life during that oppressive time lingered. Tess read Liliana's poems with grace and with informed excitement, clearly eager for us to love the poems as much as she did, and through her voice another voice, the resonance of this "new" poet, came to us – by turns sceptical, ironic, delighted, chilling, gracious, believing, unbelieving. I was impressed immediately by this voice.

And yet, when I was asked to write an introduction to a new translation of her poems, I hesitated for several reasons, not the least being that I have begun to doubt whether an appropriate tone will ever be found in English for the writings of East European poets. These presentations often seem fraught with a sanctimonious tone, or with an oil-and-vinegar mixture of humility and grandiosity, as if the introducing agent were in part responsible for liberating these poets into the promised land of an English-speaking readership. How should one behave in relation to these writers who have endured a destiny that is still unfolding, without seeming to annex their forms of suffering to our (often) different forms of suffering.

Liliana Ursu has provided a twofold answer to this. Naming certain women writers – European and American – in a brief essay entitled 'The Twice Born', she speaks of a shared quality of obsessiveness which has 'liberated them, made their lives coherent both as women and as artists, eliminated doubt'. To be among these writers, she claims, no matter what their country of origin, is to be in the company of the 'twice born'. And although she acknowledges that the poet in Eastern Europe has had a 'more exciting life' – not simply the daily hardships of standing in food lines or raising families and working under conditions of massive political repression, but also forming poems honestly and outwitting those who would suppress their truths with censorship – she writes convincingly of the great kinship she feels with such writers as Sylvia Plath, Anne Sexton, Diane Wakowski and others, and reminds us that 'the only difference between Eastern [European] poets and Western poets at the time was the free condition of the latter'.

Despite her belief in the universal dilemma of the woman writer (still !), it is unnerving to confront a full body of work such as Liliana Ursu's *The Sky Behind the Forest*, knowing what strength it must require to create, from the personal, subjective lyric, a code for freeing the individual consciousness from the conditions of a barbaric state. My favourites of these poems are the terse, shimmering, elliptical short lyrics, those of fewer than twenty lines; these speak to me deeply of the need to conserve time and space, and the need to represent wildly but accurately the conditions of a life when such representation must necessarily be symbolic. 'This line must stand for everything,' some of her poems make me think. She came of age in the seventies when much poetry – not only in Europe but also in Britain and America – became more constrained, encoded and surreal but when the tendency for newly emerging women writers was to be more passionately, morally outspoken and wildly expressive. Plath, in her fearlessness to say the unspoken and often the unspeakable, has been their strongest influence, according to Adam Sorkin, who has translated many Romanian women poets, among whom Liliana Ursu is distinguished by her passion and her often disarming tenderness.

It is this tension between not saying and saying – between the encoded, odd, often sensual suggestiveness which is testing the boundaries of prescribed action and the explosively forthright, moral element – that interests me in these compelling lyrics. Often we hear a woman speaking both inwardly and outwardly. In 'Dialogue', she writes:

> Like a mother testing hot water for her baby's bath,
> I place each letter carefully upon the page.
> How benevolent it seems, the Tower of Babel in Kafka's canvas,
> yet how terrifying the silence between bricks...

And after this, how terrifying the silence between stanzas! Such shifts – from the image of the mother testing the water, to the 'benevolence' of Kafka's tower with the mortar of silence cementing the bricks – all as an extended metaphor for the painfulness of writing – are characteristic of this poet. She can ice-skate across her subject matter and see face after face pressed up from underneath. The faster she goes in a short space, the more effective her poems are, the more enlivening the struggle between movement and the motionless. In a poem called 'Really, Don't You Believe Me?' she writes:

> On the windowsill, oranges.
> On the table, a loaf of bread, a knife,
> my children counting oranges on trees in a postcard.
>
> I climb towards the monastery
> while a hunter shoots at wild geese,
> insulting the sky...
>
> Power has no imagination.
> No need of imagination,
> not for poets,
> not for a grove of orange trees in flower...

This last stanza recalls for me Simone Weil's profound essay about the intolerable nature of power and warfare in *The Iliad*. Especially striking are the valleys between stanzas here, and the way the oranges seem to become lighter while the moral gravity and bitter irony of the statements become "heavier". At first the oranges are presented as solitary, then as part of a child's imagined landscape, and finally as sheerly beautiful, useless to the exerciser of power. And yet this 'uselessness' of the imagination enables the poet to exceed exterior power. The image is enchanting and chilling, and one can be enchanted and chilled without quite knowing what stands for what in the poem, or how carefully she must be speaking about some other subjects. It is helpful to know that oranges, which were unobtainable for most people in Romania under Ceaucescu, have a power associated with exclusion, confinement, and abundance elsewhere. In Liliana's personal case they may also represent the strictures of travel.

In another of my favourite poems in this collection, 'Season's End', she also mentions oranges in a significant way:

> O Lord, have mercy on us,
> we who are stuffed with lies.
> The wind howls through our coats, houses, pockets.
> More and more white-haired children wait in line for oranges.
>
> I wade into this age.
> Would that the waters
> could wash these years away.

In staccato rhythms, Ursu boldly makes the jump from stuffed (with lies) to starving (for oranges); the oxymoron of the patient, white-haired children is quite moving, as is the poet's plea to the power-less water; the poem closes with a violent grace: 'But our only sea is the Black Sea,/and our land, a frozen ocean.'

If such small fresh things as oranges recur with great force for this poet, it is as the wild strawberries recur for director Ingmar Bergman; there are also these summery, unexpected wild fruits in Liliana Ursu's poems, it so happens – to suggest the sustaining quality of a most enigmatic imagination, its saving strengths against some terribly unlikely odds. It's to be hoped that as her poems now reach a growing audience, they will help us all, as she implores, 'pick wild strawberries from the lip of the abyss'.

BRENDA HILLMAN

TRANSLATORS' NOTES

TESS GALLAGHER:

I first heard the poems of Liliana Ursu read by her in Romanian at the 1990 Catalonian International Poetry Festival in Barcelona. Not since the early 1970s, when I'd been swept up by the Stanley Kunitz translations of the great Russian poet, Anna Akhmatova, had I encountered a woman's voice so carnivorous and tender, majestic and human. Her poems yielded a humanly political veracity which did not accede to cynicism, but seemed to have witnessed with a clear gaze what had befallen her country, its people.

Even before I saw translations of these poems into English, I sensed from this poet's physical carriage and intonations in Romanian – a language I did not know – that I was being moved by those mysterious, inexplicable resonances which belong to voice and to spirit. '*Anima religiosa*' is a term Liliana used to describe another writer in a recent letter, but I realise this phrase beautifully applies to her own capacities. She writes from a religious soul and the sustaining elements of her poems arise from ritual and humility, from tenacious, mindful suffering and deeply held religious practices and belief. Her voice is impetuous and full of a rushing audacity that can stab the consciousness by suddenly becoming stark and acute.

The spectrum of Liliana's poetic reach combines the sensual and spiritual, the personal with the historical, the mythical with the daily. I don't know when such qualities have been so powerfully available to English-speaking readers. The jaundiced contemporary heart, closed to miracles and scant of the religious, may at least be persuaded to pause, to glimpse another world, when confronted with these poems. When Liliana speaks of 'a divine wound', the authority of her life is collateral to the utterance. The 'soul exceeding itself' is a dimension made palpable by the poet's spiritual exuberance. When she writes 'needles of ice darken my being', we cross the portal of an inner extremity in the company of one who has survived it.

I recall that some of these poems were composed on the backs of letters and poems I wrote to Liliana during subsequent paper shortages since the fall of the Ceaucescu regime. The image of that circumstantial compounding of means and energies – poems written on the backs of poems – reminds me of the fortunate conjunction of mutual gifts and rare friendship which have joined me to this important project with Liliana Ursu and Adam Sorkin.

My offering to this book has been largely that of a companioning poet whose attention to music and whose empathetic spirit may lend an already extraordinary instrument resonance in the new language. At times I have moved like an anxious mother to tear away from the poems the filmy birth-membrane which, here and there, might have obscured a poem's availability, its dramatic presence for American readers.

When I realised various syntactical changes would sharpen the pulse, we revised accordingly. We honoured Liliana's characteristically strong beginnings and endings by making sure these were as emphatic or dire in English as we knew them to be in Romanian.

For the sake of keeping the rhythmic circuitry in English as supple as it is in Romanian, the poems have needed more punctuation than Liliana sometimes used in the original English versions or in their Romanian originals. Therefore, we have applied punctuation consistently when it amplified meaning and emotion. Also, Adam and I have admitted to the poet when we just didn't "get" an image – didn't know what she meant to accomplish or communicate. With Liliana's help we have, on occasion, reformulated the image or movement until her wishes took on fresh strength in the translation. The vital nuance and mellifluous timbre of Liliana Ursu's extraordinary voice have, at all times, been our mentors.

In one of her poems Liliana refers to 'poets from opposite poles of this world'. With Adam's excellent ministrations, this book, in its substance and in the very process of its translation, represents a dialogue between those poles – English and Romanian. Many of the poems of the last section show that America has had both an uplifting and an unsettling affect upon a poet whose sensibility, courage and expectations, we must never forget, were forged during the constrictions of Communism and a maniacal dictatorship. She is a woman for whom both love and country have been precariously held in jeopardy – the 'dove's egg in a crow's beak'. In searing dramatic moments she is able to convey the despair and fortitude of her generation, as in the image of a boy in the attic playing a trumpet near his hanged father. When she gives us 'the blue-grey scream of peacocks / in Sibiu at night' it also represents the once stifled voices of a nation, what she calls elsewhere 'the carnage within'.

The narrative of this manuscript moves from interminable winter toward uneasy spring. It variegates the political with the personal,

14

first caress with corrosive dismay, betrayal and fervent spiritual outcry. The book's contraries involve images of great fragility and menace, of caresses under 'anxious wings', of swallows co-existing with eagles. This poet possesses an amazing core of lyric resilience, but it is her narrative range which allows the diamond hooves of her lyrics traction in a cosmos where the compass is always whirling.

I believe some uncanny fatedness must have honoured me with the chance to companion these poems. My friendship with Liliana came at a time when I most needed it, in aftermath to my husband, Raymond Carver's, death. Twice in 1992 I visited Romania. During sweltering July, I sat with Liliana and her family under the apple trees of the family's summer cottage in Ciorogârla, a village near Bucharest.

One night we had finished our dinner and were sitting in the coolness talking. Just outside the radius of our candlelight a stray cat appeared which had been coming nightly to be fed. It had come several evenings and now we'd begun to look forward to it. Usually we just waited for it to approach shyly, but that night I suddenly called to it, 'Come here, my Pusha!'

'What did she call it?' Liliana's father asked her.

'Pusha!' Liliana repeated incredulously, still looking at me.

'Where did she hear that word?' her father asked.

Liliana, translating, asked me if I'd ever heard the word 'pusha' before.

'No,' I said. 'It just came out of me. I thought I made it up.'

A flurry of Romanian passed as she conveyed my answer. Then she and her father exchanged exclamations of delight and awe. Finally she let me in on what they'd been saying. She explained that 'Pusha' was a Romanian endearment her father had called her as a girl.

'We don't know how you found this word,' she said.

Since that night in the orchard Liliana has allowed me to reclaim this childhood name which joins her lovingly to a time long before I knew her. Her father passed away in 1993, so the name is now importantly ghosted. I use it in letters and in moments of affection on the telephone to draw us close. But also, it keeps alive that mysterious moment in the garden where language exceeded time and space, soared eerily beyond all but mutual acceptance.

So, dear Pusha, please accept bountiful thanks for the gift of these poems – companions to their mysterious and beautiful Romanian counterparts.

Sky House, Port Angeles, WA
17 March 1995

I first met Liliana Ursu in May of 1989 when she appeared at a formal meeting in the small office of the English Department at the University of Bucharest. I had gone to Romania on a Fulbright grant to translate contemporary Romanian poetry, especially the poetry of the generation of poets that began to publish books in the 1970s. Liliana Ursu was, and continues to be, a strong and prominent voice among this group.

This gathering at the university was my first conference with those who had been proposed to collaborate with me on the translations. I had no idea who would be included. I was acquainted with most of the handful of people in the room from a prior grant, but I was quite surprised to be introduced to a vivacious, brown-haired woman who was not a member of the department. Surprised and pleased. This new person, resplendent in a flowered summer dress, spoke excellent English. She was Liliana Ursu, whose passionate lyrical works I knew, both from her own renderings in her 1982 anthology in English, *15 Young Romanian Poets*, and from Andrea Deletant and Brenda Walker's versions in their 1986 groundbreaking collection of Romanian women poets, *Silent Voices*.

Conditions in Romania in 1989 were tense and awful in every conceivable way, tangible and intangible. We were only able to meet in carefully correct and official circumstances, usually over the long table in the inner office of the two rooms shared by all department members. I'd suggested this for our meetings, since it would be a relatively safe place for my Romanian colleagues to be seen talking with me. There – with a bust of Shakespeare on the book shelf at one end of the room and, above it, the requisite framed portrait of the megalomaniac Great Conductor, Nicolae Ceaucescu, wearing a supposedly benevolent but unmistakably imperious, self-satisfied paternal grin, while exuding air-brushed health and vitality – we were able to give our attention to essential matters, like poetry.

In this bifurcated world, Liliana Ursu and I found ourselves in clear, unspoken sympathy. Exact expression and real feeling were important, though during these times we were obliged to hide them beneath the surface; false piety and meretricious devotion were immoral and dangerous to inner freedom. In our joint working sessions on poetry, I remember vividly Liliana's spirited and sensitive initial translations, her sharp and secure English, her helpfulness, and that firm and decided way, when, with a definitive gesture of her head at the end of a discussion (as at the close of many of her poems), she made a final point that was impossible to countermand. Her presence was strong, her voice resonant, even in its necessary silences.

We met again two summers later in 1991 when I returned on a follow-up grant from the International Research and Exchanges Board (IREX) to expand my work in translation. This time, in a Romania liberated from the terrorism of the dictatorship and the immediate fear of the pervasive Securitate, we were able to meet where we liked, to walk the city streets, to speak without caution, and to share a laugh, sometimes over a glass of Romanian plum brandy – *tsuica* – or of homemade wine, a pale, strong country vintage produced by Liliana's father.

On one occasion, Liliana interviewed me for the radio literary magazine she produced. She set up a portable cassette recorder in the Cismigiu Gardens near the centre of Bucharest, a beautiful, if slightly seedy, public park that reminds one of the elegance and the cosmopolitan European past which the communist government tried to eradicate. On a bench surrounded by blooming rose bushes in curlicues of garden beds, the tape reeled on under blue sky. Later we retired to a table at a closed sidewalk café nearby to go over some drafts of her poems in English. She also showed me translations of her poems she'd worked on with Tess Gallagher, whom she had met at an international poetry festival in Barcelona in 1990, a year earlier. This trip to Barcelona was only the second time she had been able to travel out of Romania, the first having been to London. Under the nation's tight restrictions on travel, until the revolution of December 1989 toppled the government, she and other writers had been held in their country. She had previously been refused permission to attend the Barcelona festival in 1986.

In late June of 1991, I was invited to a colloquium for translators and publishers of Romanian literature held in Bucharest and the nearby mountain resort of Sinaia. I then travelled north-east to Iasi and Moldavia with others, including Liliana and her son Mihnea. On this trip Liliana and I decided to collaborate on a book of translations of the poets of Sibiu – a small city located in the mountains of Transylvania, her birth place and the true home of her spirit. The dual-language collection, *Focuri pe apa / Fires on Water*, presenting seven poets, was published in the autumn of 1992 by the Cartea Româneasca (Romanian Book) Publishing House in Bucharest, in conjunction with the newly established Sibiu Poetry Centre.

During this trip we also began work on this present book of her poems, to be taken from her five previous books, from *Port Angeles*, and from new poems written since then. I should mention that the financial difficulties which have caused over three years' delay in the publication of *Port Angeles* by a struggling private firm are rather a common circumstance for many publishers in post-communist Romania, where poetry has predictably been marginalised in the new free market universe of unsubsidised publishing.

Next, in a convergence of energies destined to focus on Liliana's poems, both Tess Gallagher and I attended the European Poetry Festival held in Sibiu in October 1992. On the way, we arrived in Bucharest just in time to greet the initial copies of the Sibiu anthology, in which Tess was also represented by her translation of Liliana Ursu's poem 'Port Angeles', done with Liliana. Unfortunately, Liliana herself was in America, teaching at Penn State's main campus on a Fulbright grant, and could not be with us in Sibiu.

I had carried my work on this manuscript of Liliana's poems with me, and on the long plane trip back from Romania to New York City, Tess and I first began to look at Liliana's poems together. So yet another important layer of attention was added to this book, that of a woman poet whose empathetic, poetic and personal closeness to Liliana have hopefully allowed some poems and parts of poems to become more fully available for the reader. Although the remainder of Tess's and my work with one another has taken place through the mails and over the telephone, this initial period of time together in Liliana's birth-place, in Bucharest, and in the sky at 38,000 feet became the foundation of the three-way collaboration which produced the final shaping of this book.

Liliana and I have kept in steady contact during the five years of collaboration. I have had the good fortune to be able to work with her, both in this country, when she was here as a Fulbright lecturer in 1992, and again in the summer of 1993 in her family apartment in Bucharest. There we reviewed most of the poems in this book, adding some she had written in Pennsylvania as well as one or two more recent poems. During the year of work that followed, Tess's emphasis on several matters including clarity, syntactical emendations and factual queries necessitated that the manuscript be passed through couriers to Liliana in Bucharest, then back from her to the United States more than once.

Collaborative work can vary greatly in degree and mode. As Liliana Ursu and I initially translated together, she would offer a first version aloud, then together we would create something more than an initial rough draft. Next I'd revise and rewrite further – my Romanian-English dictionary, Webster's collegiate dictionary,

18

and Roget's all at hand. The real fun, at least for me, began as we proposed and parried terms, supplied and subtracted connotations, fitted line, honed image, listened to voice, tuned and torqued the emerging English rhythms. Finally, the integration of Tess's with Liliana's and my own efforts has, I believe, greatly strengthened the offering. Our work has been so fully surrendered to the poems that I could not say now whose suggestion became the final version.

The headnote to Liliana Ursu's English versions of her poetry in *15 Young Romanian Poets* offers her own editorially distanced description of her work. I'll conclude this note by eavesdropping on the poet's self-definition, joining with her in the third person:

> Her poems have a strong responsiveness to the inexhaustible variety and power of the visible world as perceived by an alert sensibility...her guiding principle is that every poem should be its own sole freshly-created universe...her verse is suffused with a compassionate melancholy, a sense of the transience of things, an awareness of the random quality inherent in human existence.

This rich and energetic voice is what we've aimed at bringing to English-speaking readers in the versions of her poems that follow – most of them are fairly faithful to the Romanian originals, although, hopefully, in those places where the poems needed to move differently in English, our changes will allow them to be more faithful to their initial impulses and the wider virtues of poetry.

Havertown, PA
September 1994

ABOUT THE TRANSLATORS

Adam J. Sorkin is one of America's most widely published translators of contemporary Romanian poetry. His versions of over fifty Romanian poets have appeared in many American literary magazines. His work with Liliana Ursu began in 1989. They continued, with Tess Gallagher's integral participation, to collect and refine this volume. Another collaboration with Liliana Ursu produced *Fires on Water*, a collection of poets from her birth city of Sibiu in Transylvania. With co-translators, Adam Sorkin has published three additional volumes of Romanian poetry including *Transylvanian Voices: An Anthology of Contemporary Poets of Cluj-Napoca* and *An Anthology of Romanian Woman Poets*, both in 1994. He received support from the Fulbright Scholar Program, the Rockefeller Foundation, the International Research and Exchanges Board, and the European Association for the Promotion of Poetry. Sorkin is a Professor of English at Penn State Delaware Country Campus.

Tess Gallagher, a poet, short story writer and essayist, was allowed time to collaborate on this translation work with Liliana Ursu and Adam Sorkin by a Lyndhurst Prize awarded in 1993. The three-year stipend especially encourages development in new directions. Her most recent books are: BRITAIN: *My Black Horse: New and Selected Poems* (1995) and *Portable Kisses* (1996), both from Blood-axe Books; USA: *Portable Kisses Expanded* (Capra Press, 1994), and the Classic Edition of *Instructions to the Double*, reissued by Carnegie Mellon in 1994. Her *Moon Crossing Bridge* (Graywolf, 1992) received American Library Association recognition as one of two best books of poetry in America that year. Tess Gallagher's first book of short stories, *The Lover of Horses*, was reissued by Graywolf Press in 1992. Her essays are collected in *A Concert of Tenses* (University of Michigan Press, 1986). She co-authored two screenplays with her husband Raymond Carver, and after his death contributed to the making of the Robert Altman film *Short Cuts,* based on Carver's work. Tess Gallagher has also written introductions to books such as *All of Us: The Collected Poems of Raymond Carver* (Harvill, 1996). Her second book of short stories, *At the Owl Woman Saloon*, is forthcoming in autumn 1977 from Scribners.

1 *In the Forest*

In the Forest

(after Henri Rousseau)

I wrote the essential poem on an oar
just before setting out.
Perhaps long ago it's been erased
or maybe the sea
knows it now
by feel.

Like the woman in Rousseau's painting
I shudder
at the sound of footsteps
– when fear comes on too strong.

The path I follow
is a knife blade.
Maybe this is why
the sky behind the forest
is now so red.

I wrote the essential poem on an oar,
just before setting out.

Title It As You Like

One suspects a beautiful woman
of almost anything
except poetry.

By tradition women poets are homely.
Otherwise you can't believe in them;
art requires selflessness, solitude, crises, complexes,
glasses with very thick lenses, and of course
teenage acne – a sign of purity
and intense dreaming confined by four walls.

You feel obliged to flirt with a beautiful poet,
to polish her verses,
to suggest other lines of work.
And besides, beauty impresses fools.
A beautiful poet makes critics
more cynical, suspicious, finicky.

One suspects a beautiful woman
of almost anything.
But poetry.

Season's End
(for Mirela)

This age I'm living through with near indifference,
like a lizard that's left one more skin behind,
sunning myself on a deserted beach in the last of summer sun,
ready, with my trivial store of physical and psychic powers,
to consign myself to winter...
'Yes, sir, you're right – to each age its satisfactions.'

Well, this isn't the place to complain about petty fears,
or about your lifeless TV set.

Since I've stood in this line so long, I guess I'll buy
even fatty meat.

'The sky begins at your ankles,' whispers a dying poet,
secluded in a provincial cinema.

We're for dialogue, not violence!

A bird skims the water.
O Lord, have mercy on us,
we who are stuffed with lies.
The wind howls through our coats, houses, pockets.
More and more white-haired children wait in line for oranges.

I wade into this age.
Would that the waters
could wash these years away.
But our only sea is the Black Sea,
and our land, a frozen ocean.

Unforgetting

Between us
I pile up snow,
I pile up silence.
And no one in this city knows
why it's such a hard winter.
My angels
drink whiskey from wine glasses
and forget to forget you.
Music falls
softly onto my eyelids.
This hour, a startled bird
perches as in a monastery,
within walls
you've built
to contain me.
And I,
a soldier, obedient
to my solitude,
sleep a white sleep…

Rain in Sibiu

Rain in Sibiu, rain white, grey, black – the sky
an impenetrable safe.
All along our fence they bloom,
the white keepsake flowers
called in Romanian 'Coins of Pity'.
On the street a brass band parades for a wedding or maybe a funeral.

Strange – those monotonous rains –
sometimes grey, sometimes white, and even black.
There was something about them, something cheap and dreary
like the stiff body of a dog in the dew-covered grass
or the interminable grinding of the hurdy-gurdy in films about Paris.

Even now I wake up in the dead of night,
rain streaming down my shoulders
and Johan's son above me in the cold attic,
still playing desperately on his trumpet
beside his hanged father.

Seascape

You, the technocrat who killed yourself in an elevator,
your only witness an empty beer bottle
while the sea, always extending the landscape,
licks our souls greedily,
fed up with algae, with bones, with ultimate questions.

Tonight the world's brain rises, hisses
carnivorously: The Moon!
'Oh no,' whisper the lovers, who spend everything –
it's a coin rolling from the pocket of the drowned.

Poem with a Griffin, a Pike and Peacocks

I'm reading a poem while it rains.
The day blinks
through windows guarded by a griffin; its talons
flex, its tail switches.

Do you remember those summer showers high in the mountains?
The dull pop of a toadstool beneath your bare foot
in the dew-covered grass?

Under a crystal bell jar, the still life – fleshy ripe bananas,
cherries, lemons and the silver knife you bargained for in the bazaar
as the Bosphorus sparkled at the feet of the one you loved.
On the wobbly kitchen table, with that very knife,
you slit open a pike.

And the hunting rifle, propped against stuffed peacocks –
has it turned into a lapdog
licking the other woman's hands
as she weighs my pearls...?

You Haven't a Face

You haven't a face. No words
on your tongue. You are an isthmus.
A banquet table of fir afloat
in a shadowy woods.
The sun rises from you,
burning away mists that cling to my body.

You raise a conch in your hands
and it spires to the sky,
an astral silence.
A dew drop on my nipples,
a new moon around my thighs – your kisses
on my arms are crushed wild strawberries.
A cosmic shudder, my love.

Love is blind.
Love is blind.
Only our mouths see.

Double Portrait

In the background: the lake, pine trees, deliberate stillness.
In the foreground: the photographer (a sports jacket, a red pullover)
and the indifferent dog.
Famous and ageless, she is about to smooth her hair with her hand –
but instead she bites into an apple.

The lake is frozen. Under its whiteness: hunger –
under the expensive blouse: another hunger.
Suddenly she slips back to the crowded suburb,
to the girl collecting wash from a line in winter,
her frozen camisole, her flashlight
illuminating the endless rope,
her cheap blouse half-open
under his feverish fingers.

And now in the sun's intense light,
her glasses steaming opaque, she remembers –
and the photographer: 'Redo your makeup. A step forward, please,
so the villa, so the border of primroses can be seen!'

A step backwards, yes, as far as possible from that girl.

Contre Jour

*'A woman made this film
against*

*the law
of gravity'*

– ADRIENNE RICH

My heart to the wall
in the room with plastic flowers.
My body shut in your body
like a divine wound
so close so far so deep
only my head against the back-lighting
and you don't know it's me any more
and you rush elsewhere
into another body

Evening after Evening

Evening after evening, she polishes the stove until it glows.
Then one day somebody whispers something into her ear.
She throws a shawl over her shoulders
and rushes to the river.

Now the stove is black, black
and nobody wants to bathe in that river anymore.

But oh how radiantly the river has begun to shine,
since that certain day.

If Night Weren't So Long

If night weren't so long
I wouldn't have to make myself beautiful.
I wouldn't spend hours before the mirror putting on makeup,
I wouldn't try on dress after dress
or reproach the telephone
for its stubborn game with silence.

I'd telephone you
without makeup,
with eyes reddened by tears,
with an unwritten letter in my hand,
naked in the abyss of the room.
I'd telephone you
after that first time
you didn't come —
If night weren't so long.

Moment with Thunder

(for Tess)

In full winter the mountain sky lightened,
then green thunder somersaulted into the white abyss
like the torrent of a waterfall in summer
near which one can hardly breathe,
thrilled to be so close
to that tumbling down of wings,
your own soul exceeding itself,
its single white candle aflame
in the translucent skies of an angel.

Once, in summer, at Sirnea in the mountains
I was reading from Thomas Mann.
It was a doubtful season among mists,
a shy sun hazing through, when I first heard it –
a moan, then a rustling behind me
like the noise made by a lizard quickening in grass.
I turned and saw it, the newborn
lying under the hot, rough tongue
of its mother, busy over its stillness, the kid
gushing red against her white flank like a tiny clown
turned to stone in that immensity of grass.

Blinded by their moment of darkness, I stumbled down the path.
On my way I met two children
carrying a bucket of water between them
from the river. I was going down; they
were going up to their older sister
who was washing her hair in the mountains.
'Her name is Orange,' said the boy.
'And her hair is so long,' the girl added, 'it can surround
this whole mountain!'
'But what are your names?' I asked.
'Apple and Peach,' their answer came –
the same instant as the thunder.

The Goldsmiths' Market

How these early dawns loom, full of curiosity, at the windows
of poets and goldsmiths!
In their cramped workshops in the tower they distill snowflakes,
delicate meadows of violets, the perfume of whispering.
Whispers?
Whose whispers?
The goddess with the airy steps,
the photographer or the hunter
as they ready themselves for love.
Next the burnishing of metal until they lose their sight,
sometimes until they lose their minds.

Just beyond their shop door a newborn kid rises bleating –
life itself flourishes, propels poet and alchemist
into the splashing river
where silver trout glint a dream-like memory of flesh.
Along the banks cherry trees hang heavy with promises,
plump cherries they can never reach.

How the last moments of dusk linger, full of curiosity
           at their windows,
while the smiths of word, of gold
lure reality with a luminous kernel of light.

And the kid sinks to sleep on a cloud...

Flowers of the Pyre

Flowers of the pyre, wild force within the delicate petals
bursting even from parched rock.
And the funeral fire, simple, final. Dark, dark.
'Roses for sale! Buy my roses!
Roses for sale! Roses!' The girl with golden thighs entices...
Death himself could fall for her.
'Beauty isn't for just anyone,' your smile hints to me
as you shake the stopped watch.
But then who'd buy her roses
if she cried out, offering them in their truest name?

'Flowers of the pyre...death's fire-flowers,' the poet murmurs softly
wandering through the goldsmiths' market of the ancient town.

Spring in Dream

In spring everything begins and ends in dream.
I used to come to your mother's house, so shy, so much in love.
You were never there, in the room with the piano and the freesias.
Under my eyes the score of Chopin's *Preludes* trembled
from our first unexpected meeting.

Before my piano lesson
she'd slip the rings from my fingers.
'The hand must be free when it touches the keys.
Must fly. A ring is too heavy a burden, a disequilibrium.
A false note in art as in life.'

Once in a dream we were on a Japanese island
in a bare room near a blue fire
beside which I was taking off my clothes.
We were separated by a white silk screen
– plum trees in flower and a waterfall
on which the shadow of my body fell in sharp silhouette.
It was then you first touched me,
resting your forehead against the cool silk of the screen.
When the silk started to burn under your hands –
long ago – I had already vanished.

The Comet Is Coming

You were writing, your glasses fogged over.
Only your smile was still vibrant
among the houses, the blue streets before an endless field.
'The comet is coming! The comet is coming!' the children cheered,
and everybody looked up.
Hunched over the earth, you were pulling weeds
while your jerky writing slowly faded from my letter.
'What a strange dream,' people exclaim, tearing at the lilac bush,
a dead comet tangled in its branches.

Indeed, what a strange dream.

Portrait

Don't let yourself be cheated by soft red lips,
a smile's sweet swindle.
Black nothingness lurks a hair's-breadth behind your back.
'Your humble servant, ladies and gentlemen,
your good angel! My poem won't suck your blood.
Tempt your hearts a little with an illusion –
the reconciling of spirit and flesh.'

(Two birds are slaughtered beneath your window.
The shadow steps closer, closer.)

I was dreaming of dolphins and palm trees.
Why did you wake me?

2 *With One Eye We Cry, With the Other We Laugh*

With One Eye We Cry, with the Other We Laugh

Romanians don't have a statue of liberty,
its nearness to the ocean.
We have scythed grass,
uniforms that changed overnight.
Slender candles flicker
above our martyrs,
and even those are few.

The national theatre is close by:
if we were to cry out, Medea would answer;
if we whisper, Avram Iancu prompts us in our parts.
Both angel and devil are locked in the prompter's box.

Romanians don't have a statue of liberty
but maybe we have a star of liberty,
and maybe we have an underground theater,
a president costumed in the glare of grease-paint,
the Goddess of Justice standing over him,
completely blind, holding her crooked balance.
Isn't this theatre, O God, an upside-down sky?

With one eye we cry, with the other we laugh,
on the other side of liberty

Silent Voices

(for Cella Delavrancea and Gabriela Melinescu)

They descend many times a day, each
to her own hell – paltry, stately, matter-of-fact –
O pure spirit!
the iron ivy of words
blooms, then withers over their poverty-stricken mouths.
Others make book on them,
bet as if on horses;
they have red hair, chestnut, are splendid in their flesh, in their
        despair.
In flowered dresses they keep dancing, keep loving;
they cross oceans with no life preserver.

They are like priestesses of a church, its thick walls,
the smoke of glances – they are subdued,
prayerful, unconquerable – the hush
of their white hair.
Their souls pass through walls
smiling at the seven deadly sins
painted in naive icons.
The ropes of the big bell have chafed prayer into their flesh.
Submerged in their blood, books circulate – on the pillow
the moon rests. Atrocious
and black. Proud as a black woman's breast.

So long, death!

Black claws press into their
palms. Requiems. Each like a scarf
tattered with signs.

Submerged in professional indulgence,
even their own blood has turned professional
in their fight with fever, with inertia, with the atom bomb,
with their own sex.

The film continues.
Parallel sequences:

in her mountain village
leaning over the deep well,
she turns the winch
and the moon spins.
What a dizzy wreath, remembrance over an abyss!
The fragile smile of Ophelia rises from the old mother-water
while the Fates, women themselves, inscribe destiny into the sky,
the lines of the palm – inscribing hate, generosity, and three or
        four dreams...

The 97-year-old writer climbs the steps with support.
All the lights blaze in her honor.
From every mirror Old Age ripens.
The literary world is buzzing:
some ask about her latest novel,
some the amount of her prize, some yawn snobbishly
and two or three simply don't understand
how it's possible to receive prizes when you're over 90.
'We'll never attain such an age,' says a playwright with indignant
        hiccuping.
On the piano her cherished carnations wait.
'Ah, those battles with flowers that used to take place on the
        boulevards of my youth.'
Another three steps and she's there.
'Smile, smile, don't let yourself down!'
In his rubber boots, Ion, the janitor, still smelling of fish,
arrives with the award at the last minute.
The champagne is served immediately,
and she plays Chopin: 'I shall play you a melancholy prelude and
        a gay mazurka.'
A sunbeam has stolen into her hair.
'I loved a lot,' she thinks to herself, 'and in the end that's
        what matters.'
Courageously, in her 90s, she attacks a waltz.

With silent voices they sing,
they defend themselves, admit faults, give blood,
swear at the dark, at the light.
And still –
there are more such women
eager to be born.

The Mirror's Hide and Seek

Sometimes you hide
as though behind a hideous secret.

Whose breath sets the weather cock of your heart awhirl?
Battle cries harnessed to the heavy wagons
of the real. And the word, an umbilical cord
cinched like a noose
around the facts of life, lived or merely dreamed.

The carnage within takes an instant,
a quick turn of the page for the pianist,
a mere glimpse of the postman through the steamy window.
An instant to refill the fountain pen, to light a cigarette.

The blood's assault on life in the instant of a newborn's cry.
And in the selfsame commodious moment the Nobel Prize
is awarded to the octogenarian poet;
shading his eyes from the glare of lights,
he makes his way to a podium still pungent
with the sacrificial aroma of young, resinous trees.
'Take your time, Sir! Maestro, breathe deeply!
Just another step. There you are!'
He can hardly see to write, yet his muse won't leave him alone.
Always peering over his shoulder
– an indelible shadow on every page.
A cigarette between his fingers burns to a long, grey ash.
A soughing through the conservatory gardens, a whisper.
Tomorrow it's the equinox – spring once more:
he'll have to set in a fresh bed of mint.

Woman from Sibiel in Phoenix

Around her neck she wore a tiny pouch of earth from Sibiel
She no longer knew her name in Phoenix,
or how old she'd become among foreigners.
All she could remember was a train heavy with logs,
a girl dancing the *hora*, a field of clover,
the joyous screams of the boys
when they got off the boat in New York.

The statue of liberty also wears a pouch of earth around her neck...

Now the old woman sits on a plastic chair crocheting
near a plastic table,
a plastic TV set flickering before her.
She even longs for a plastic heart
because the old one made of flesh isn't good for anything.
Here in the desert the wind howls with madness –
cactus in the garden.
If she were to cry out in her own tongue, who would come
              to help her?
As for her children, well, they are fine and healthy
in Houston, in Dallas.

After a few days, the neighbors discovered her eyes fixed
on an icon from Sibiel, and clutched in her hand
a tiny pouch of dirt...

Humility

'Each in his cell, thinking of the key'
— T.S. ELIOT

Here, the word
adrift
in the ancient blood.
There, the tedious glow of night.
Only the dancer's mouth is alive,
brazenly made–up
like a knife gash,
and her swirling skirt,
fierce savagery of green,
of crushed lilacs.

Oh, the acrobats, how they pray
to the statues of wax,
their burned hands beseeching.

Spanish Flashback
(for Tess)

We picked forget-me-nots on the highest hill of Barcelona,
took photographs of each other among clouds and snack bars,
our past already imprinted on these images.

We climbed, we descended.
Up to the Museum of Arms
up to Miró's house
up to the *sea*
and we let ourselves be filmed
by noisy French wedding attendants
who'd just stepped out of a red pullman.
(We were proud and happy in our anonymous presence:
who would have guessed we were poets from opposite poles
        of this world?)
We felt happy, suddenly protected among those travellers
lost in their *joy*, and I could almost see them later
in their twilight homes
looking at the videotape, naively pointing to us,
explaining to their friends: 'these were two nice foreigners
from the top of the hill,'

and finally our descent through the valley of green light
and Spanish souvenirs –
how brightly we mixed poetry and reality into those days

the new year's eve in Puerta del Sol
another chimera for us
when, there in the middle of our lives, we tried
with our burnt lips
to catch all twelve of that year's fiery grapes

For Constantin Noica

You feel cold.
You felt cold.
You've constantly been cold.

Locked in a room without windows
the way they punished you as a child.
You couldn't escape the cold.
Your room as a student, always an attic
or a basement.

That cell they kept you in for six years
– without a trial, a political prisoner –
you shivered from cold,
especially after torture,
when water turned to ice in your cup.
How thirsty they made you
and what could you swallow but the dark?

Still you've never been quite so cold
as when you came home,
free.
You entered a deserted house.
She'd gone away, taken your two children
leaving no address...

The last photos catch you
in your tiny room
high in the mountains at Paltinis,
a coat thrown like a cape over your shoulders.
Colder, ever colder, sitting on the narrow bed covered with books,
a board across your knees, composing
the earthly 'Treatise on Angels'.

Really, Don't You Believe Me?

On the windowsill, oranges.
On the table, a loaf of bread, a knife,
my children counting oranges on trees in a postcard.

I climb towards the monastery
while a hunter shoots at wild geese,
insulting the sky...

Power has no imagination.
No need of imagination,
not for poets,
not for a grove of orange trees in flower,
not for monasteries –
really, don't you believe me?

But we are the *number*
and the *number*, as the philosopher wrote, is a pulsation, a throb
across this stone-cold cosmos...

Poem for a Brother in Spirit

You commute between Long Island, Sulmona, Sarmizegetusa.
You play the waiter on the small ferryboat, make plans
for Ovid, that he will at last return
from Constantsa to his native Sulmona
on a sailing ship at the end of the twentieth century.
You were paid to keep silent;
paid all that time just to exist, to churn out films
and never expected that soon you'd be jogging
between two worlds, soon you would lose the marathon.

Alone for Easter, alone for Christmas,
each weekend a Sahara
you write poems about your desk lamp filled with pennies
and who knows why you suddenly yearn for the new Tulburel wine
and suddenly over your shoulder yearn for yourself.

Here, in Bucharest, the snow has begun to melt.
Everything is muddy and obscure.
Chimney sweeps find little work;
we buy endless newspapers, we feed on newspapers,
our intestines gurgle with so many news items and lies,
so many half-digested truths.

Ovid is still in Constantsa.
The Dacians' Sarmizegetusa is dreamed of only by you
there in the belly of Manhattan.
'An upside-down world,' says the philosopher, in line for meat.

Above the Bridge

Above the bridge that no one crosses anymore,
something remains in the mist of September:

near – the white monastery, geraniums,
prayers overheard, the lightning toll of the great bell;

far – a smile, my tongue discovering
the lines of solitude on your silent palm.

Above the bridge that no one crosses any more...

Portrait with Dandelions

The two lovers take their amusement, their glasses always filled.
They kiss, they embrace.
The hotel rattles under the beating of their huge wings.
'Something comes near, nearer. Perhaps it's love?'
he asks himself. 'Perhaps death?'
He combs her hair over his weary knees.

And she, really crying, hidden behind thronging wings
– or another tale about great love, how it begins
or ends. Really crying.

3 *Bait*

Bait

The boy keeps his fishing bait
in his grandfather's pewter cigarette-case.
Inside it, the muted world it reflects –
a battle front, love, nerves which surrendered
propelling the old man into the emptiness of the lake.
Patiently, the boy is waiting for fish
while the cigarette-case,
tipped open in the grass,
fogs him over heavily with dew.

Casual Event

Needles of ice darken my being.
A hunter passes and waves. Tossed
over his shoulder – fresh pelts, still steaming.
A handful of birds peck at corn meal
we've scattered over the ice:
gold to their day, gold!

Beneath us the green going of the river
and the fish, which no longer rise.
The line from the rod, stretched taut, cuts us asunder,
a barrier cleaving life and death –
at its end, definitive and final, lead.
Then a sudden struggle echoes in the blood,
at one with my very pulse.
A small fragment of the world –
this roiling circle of water.

Life Under Ground

As if in an underground cathedral swarming with pilgrims,
he sits stone still, his hands in his lap, legless
on his wooden dolly small as a book.
From a distance he seems an idol of darkness,
the way he faces the broad stairwell as if toward a sacred sea –
eyes transfixed by nothingness, oblivious of the hurried passersby
pouring into the subways and out, as if
from the frenzied cement-mixers of destiny.

He doesn't utter a word, he doesn't beg, he doesn't implore, he
          won't thank anybody –
he simply sits like the hub of the surging crowd, motionless,
insignificant, beyond tragic...
Above him, a young man stands erect,
eyes lost in *Phenomenology of the Spirit*, ice skates
draped casually over one shoulder.

Orpheus

Your eyes, so clouded by journeys,
have beaten paths into the sky
and buried love in Hell.

Between the terraces of the city and the bus terminal
a saxophone mourns, keening above
the dawn path you opened through the snow,
always on the lookout for love – *'insieme, sempre insieme!'*

From my window I can see only the tops of the leafless poplars,
abandoned nests and satellite dishes.
The grass and flowers remain below, far away,
like the sky and the blue of your eyes...

I've crammed myself so full of lies it's no wonder
I failed to save my love from Erebus.
His disconsolate head and lyre still illuminate the world's seas.
I'd give anything to be the measuring pan balanced on its chains
under the cargo of your tireless heart, to feel
with what an awful weight it pulls downwards,
Orpheus.

Dialogue

(to Emil Cioran)

Like a mother testing hot water for her baby's bath,
I place each letter carefully upon the page.
How benevolent it seems, the Tower of Babel in Kafka's canvas,
yet how terrifying the silence between bricks...

I was talking with a philosopher about poetry
and a poet about philosophy,
when the boy with a nervous flashlight jammed the airwaves,
a ham radio operator who knows nothing, nothing
about either philosophers or poets
since he trades in other inflections, words netted
from the ether (what a word! what a word! winding crazily like
            a wayward path,
yet always pointing the same direction,
a runnel dug by rain into mountains, by shepherds and sheep),
and time murdered, an exquisite corpse
propped on its side against a lighthouse –
as a friend, poet or philosopher, might fancy.

'Compassion is the name for grace,' you wrote to me beside your
            waterfall,
deafened by its silence...
Oh, the strategies of pleasure on the panoramic screen of the heart!

In the midst of the carnival I find myself the only masquerader
            without a mask
and am granted no forgiveness.
Zola the photographer isn't so well known here
as Zola the writer.
That negative of me at the carnival appears in his exhibit.
An angelic collector has printed my smile anew –
it's closed under his wing – no, under his arm now, as he descends
the Fingerling Steps towards the Goldsmiths' Market.
Still on Spine of the Dog Street, the exiled philosopher
mutters from his Parisian garret: 'So – after such mockery, death!'

In the City of What Once Was

In the city of what once was, my brother tamed Sundays,
and when he no longer could, when he no longer could,
he'd gouge the shadows from the walls
with the quicks of his nails.
In the city of what once was, I repaired clocks,
and high in the tower I set the heavy iron hand
to the fragile hours.
You would pick wild strawberries from the lip of the abyss.

A word, and we came crashing down.

History of a Couple

The blue-grey scream of peacocks
in Sibiu at night.
Somewhere the sun is bloated with snores and diffuse jazz,
while a saxophone tiptoes, tiptoes
– a drum like an ice cube clinking against glass –
and the musicians' cold shadows sink deeper
under snow, deeper.
An enraged lion rips my wistful flesh.

Anatomy of a December Night

We bought the Christmas tree at the railway station
from a drunken worker: 'Since I missed the train,
I'll get home too late. Just give me what I paid for it.'
The night is darker for men like him,
illuminated by cheap drink.

On our way home you talk to me about the beautiful
and the sublime. And that worker's hands,
his blackened nails, as he handed us the fir tree,
hands, like him, humbly resigned to fate.

We shall decorate it, cover it
with cascades of silver, we'll drown sadness.
Yes, ornaments, spangles. Immaculate snow
shall cover his hands – we'll forget him.

He in the manger contentedly asleep,
you whispering in my ear: *Are we ready to face
the beautiful and the sublime?*

Above the clouds I'm happy at last.
But above the solid rock of mountains
I begin to doubt;
suddenly a tiny fire down below troubles me.
Among the fir trees life goes on.
The landing gear lowers (ah, the voluptuousness of technical terms)
the saving wheels that will force me back to the ground,
away from you.

In the night of Saint Andrew – patron of the wolves –
he gathers all the beasts before him and grants them each their prey,
all the animals they will kill in the year to come.
And none may eat more or less
than he metes out.

From now on your eyes, your hands, your mouth mete out
my power, my joy, my doubt –
Anyway, on the other side of love we're no longer alive – such
        easy prey
for words, for frost.

Contrasts

We go to look at the dead fish.
They are trucking them to the outskirts of the city:
there, once more, they'll be our quicksilver messengers
          to the underground.
The poet, your double, wheels an invalid's chair along the shore
under the moon, across his former lover's shadow,
over the confetti, onto the photograph album.
And these chimeras, scarcely restraining their laughter beneath
          transparent veils,
will soon be dead like the fish, x-rayed, enumerated,
always overexposed.

How reassuring to feel it, there in your breast pocket –
the stab of the fir tree's needle.

A Midwinter Night's Dream

I look for spring's vapour trail in an open patch of sky,
in your eyes, in the anxiety of a lifeless letter,
the pages where I pressed the splayed petals of the anemone once.
Long ago, its scarlet paled into winter.
Your tongue upon my wound traces a detour around grief.
So suddenly – riches!

From the Angel's Window

Sweet hay, raw grass, the hot udder, wild strawberries,
a green corridor, pine pitch, the cathedral.
From time to time an apple drops –
a baptism.

Through the art gallery, the girl walks by in mauve.
You skate on a frozen tear.

Da capo

Diana's Shadow

I honour you not with roses plaited in my hair
or with burning flambeaux.
I gather indifferently these few stalks of summer dill
to celebrate you this day.
The Sabbath radiance on my face
is illusion. I turn drowsy
gazing at your huntress' profile,
fall asleep at your feet
until your dogs pursue me into sunrise.

O, like these pressed blossoms still haunted by the sun,
this body once knew happiness.

The Poet's Cat

Indolent and aloof, the orange tabby
drapes herself over a pile of records.
Her yawn swallows a sunbeam
and her mistress's sleepless nights.
Her instinct for hunting is fully atrophied,
her sense of loneliness, fully indulged.

Bison Hunting

You place your foot on its neck which is bubbling
with blood. You are victory itself, you
in your light blue summer dress.
Haven't you got used to it yet?
Don't you feel its massy weight against your breasts?
Who is looking at whom from the ground?
Only blood like a green, green sea provoking you,
always the same blood, tidal, unrelenting.

Night is falling. At last your shadows superimpose
precisely.

In the Dusk

In the dusk the statues smile more enigmatically.
Not a breath of wind troubles their gaze.
You look at me and know how autumn makes its way.

In the dusk, under our bodies the hill sinks to ruin –
weightless, at last.

4 *Letter from the Constellation of the Swan*

Letter from the Constellation of the Swan

(for Cathy and Donald)

Once upon a time, maybe two weeks,
maybe two centuries ago in Pennsylvania,
a friend telephoned:
'All evening I heard a strange rustling,
as if someone were trying out
the word *sadness* in all the languages of the world.
I raised my eyes to the sky.
Wild geese were returning.
Flocks of swans followed
in solemn stateliness. I had gone out into my yard
into the soft breezes of spring
to hang the communion linen to dry.
You know the priest gives it to me
for washing.'

In this tender night of the mystical Spring of Healing,
from my window in Bucharest,
I look up to the Constellation of the Swan.
And suddenly Europe and America are fused
under wing beats, under the cosmic telescope
with which I magnify my still falling tear
toward the undying of my dear father.

Is This Wisdom?

The scent of lilac snarls into air.
With wisdom and resignation you stare at the sunrise.
Suddenly, in the crowd behind you,
you feel the flame of those black eyes,
eyes you used to love.
Your hair is grey now, your legs always cold,
your hands aching for the warmth of other hands,
hardly daring to remember how you let them go.
So, you have arrived – at wisdom?

Blues

A profusion of lilies, these accomplices of your insomnia.
You languish in a house with too many maps,
armoured by solitude.
Companioned by the self-portrait in your mirror,
you swear at her, slap her, then clasp her tenderly to your breast.
Too well you know she won't ever let you down.

And the hill, the old steeple and the newborn lambs
more delicate than the grass, but stronger than you –
are they all mere invention? And whose?
In this mood you fling the key
through the one window left open for you.
From now on you will know the sun only
through solitude's eyes.

Those young boys were dancing the *syrtaki, syrtaki*
in a Timisoara pub. Their dance
gathered momentum in the night, *syrtaki*,
tipsy and sorrowful,
but we were the night itself.

Between love's sumptuous legislation and the place you left empty
the deceitful blues of the body once again steal forth,
those torments from which you had just broken free.

Couple

She sweeps the floor. He reads the newspaper.
She washes the dishes. He reads the newspaper.
She cries. He reads the newspaper.
She screams. He reads the newspaper.
He dies. She reads the newspaper.

The Moon

Proud breast in the chill nucleus of the night,
illusion through which I make confession to autumn.
No one knows you better than this poplar,
this vacant plot of earth,
this hyacinth,
this telephone.

You are an orange tree draped in snow,
a mask abandoned in the sky,
cotton candy hawked at the fair of the human condition,
a wheelchair for an angel
or maybe an immense balloon.
The earth, invisibly attached, is your gondola-car,
weighing you down.

O moon, o bored mystery.

The Eye of the Swan
(for Nancy and Adam)

The first skyscraper is reflected in it:
the Tower of Babel.
The first fish swims in it:
the word.

Here on a college campus bearing the name of an Indian tribe
I look through many windows:
the window of Merwin,
the window of Rich,
the window of Brueghel,
the window of Chagall.

What do I see?
Yes, what do you see? the swan also asks.

I see four boulders buried in red leaves over the still green grass.
A small bird keeps hopping on one of them,
a kind of shrivelled Prufrock.
I see violet gloves
tossed hurriedly across a pair of binoculars
in a nonexistent room.

But how, in what way do I go on existing here?
– here on the Delaware campus
sealed up as if in a pyramid
and dreaming of a carefree girl in Sibiu running along a street
with brick houses and eyes staring from their roofs instead
        of windows,
shadowed by a white cat that has no feelings...

O blessed light,
come to illuminate
this Indian drum
on which a painted eagle dives –
and also frightened swallows.
Calm them,
admit them into your cathedral,
and caress the down under their anxious wings.

Tell them you exist for them only,
tell them I am milky whiteness as before,
newly risen from the mists of insomnia, innocent
as a flower under first snow
in November.

A bird strikes itself against the car's windshield.
'An unforeseeable crime,' says Adam,
taking me to see a real sequoia
shivering with birds.
He lights another cigarette.
Its tiny flame looms
and suddenly I realise night has fallen.

When I get home
the first thing I do
is draw the curtains shut.
Now only the red electronic eye of the answering machine
illuminates the monotony of objects, the feelings
that enclose me.
I start the tape:
'Liliana, what a shame you're not here.
Je suis triste à mourir.
I am alone in a motel room near Kennedy Airport.
Don't worry about me – tomorrow night I'll be reading poems
            in London. Tess.'

The next evening in Havertown I turn on a light
and take into my arms
a swan of clay.
'It's like holding a newborn,' Nancy tells me, rising
from her piano, disturbing the air
with the flame of her cheeks, almost a young girl then.
But she slips away from her tenderness, adds quietly,
'Nostalgia falsifies reality.'

But doesn't reality falsify nostalgia? I ask myself,
transforming it into a dragon which drives out the beauty memory
            insists on
or even worse, forces what was real into its surrogate,
a lukewarm cup of decaffeinated coffee.

In the eye of the swan
I see myself in Bucharest nursing my son at my breast,
I see my mother waltzing,
I see the frozen lake of Cismigiu
on which I used to skate as a child.

A pale glow gathers at the window sill
like a flute playing all on its own
at the rim of the sea. I shut my eyes and I can see light.
I open them and it's dark.

Only the eye of the swan
never closes
on light
on dark.

Spring Circumstance

a wild cherry fallen into whitewash
    or
a dove's egg in a crow's beak

Death in Spring

Just like me they try
to build shelter
in impossible places:
the outside ledge of
a casement window
thrown open every day.
Or each spring, the tree
the cats use
to sharpen their claws.
One after the other
they return with a burden of straw
or a leaf.
Only once did they succeed –
the time they built their nest in the vines
enshrouding my house.
It was turning dark slowly, sadly,
when among the black leaves I noticed
the star in their nest.

This solitary,
this neurotic spring,
forever marooned on its nest –
a bird of ice.

Ancient and Beautiful as the Mist

I dreamed I was home in Bucharest.
All day I've lived inside this dream,
clung to it, wrapped myself in it,
let myself be loved by a landscape.

How am I to convey my dream beyond the night woods
and not lose it to another dream?

Close by the stove you read Cavafy
while outside, the grass yellows under my feet.
The sea has turned white, almost a prisoner in this poem.

Only you and those books of poetry have not grown weary.
From the garden you brought me an apricot
and a butterfly drowned in the lake,
sad, dreaming of its death
on the back of my hand –
on my hand that knows you so well
though it has never caressed you.

The tenderness of your smile when you open a book –
the perfume of a ripe strawberry near which I want
to kneel.

Port Angeles

This name will first remind you of a combination
of Port Said and Los Angeles,
something exotic and unreachable, or so lost
you believe even its negative side is redeemable.
It will bring to your mind and soul the love
of the sea, yachts, palm trees, race cars,
and the night clubs you've been dreaming of
in your cheap lives.

Or you will suddenly remember a small cinema
with a pianist playing old-fashioned songs
between the newsreel about the first world war
and the film; meanwhile you'll realise
how dumb your heart has become
like an actor bandaged to the screen
during this puzzle that is life at the end of our century
after the clod-crusher of communism rolled over
Eastern Europe. 'Let us go to bed earlier tonight
because tomorrow a new world begins,' whispered
a princess with battered lips, after tortures –
But didn't Drieu La Rochelle teach us that
'The idea is always craving for blood?'
What about art? Art like faith starts with liberty.
Oh, how I craved it – *Libertate* – even before I was born...

'So what really matters is not the candle, its waxy trace,
but the light.'
And this will suddenly remind you of El Greco's angels,
of his trace in yourself. And you'll mimic that flamenco
on the patio of his memorial house in Toledo.

Oh, my drunken heart, to what dangers you give me
and in what beauty I am bathed!
Port Angeles or the zoom-effect
through which I get closer to the angels, their port.

'Don't cry, Sancho, your master is not dead!'
and for a thousandth time the sky begins in Port Angeles
where my poet friend is still watching and describing a star
that exploded 400,000 years ago,
in the Constellation of the Swan.

And now information arrives from Eastern Europe's data bank:
'Two blind men tried to cross the Danube swimming
because they chose freedom. One made it. The other
screamed with joy
when he touched shore,
but it was the wrong shore, the one he'd just left,
so instead of freedom
he was shot in the head.'

They managed to save from the tormented ocean
the astronauts who stepped onto the moon.
The people in Port Angeles were watching them on TV
while I was taking a walk under their windows
happy, bathed in wide shafts
of moonlight through hemlock.

Poem for Tess

Once, you bought a horse, in Toledo,
it was made of wood and had a warrior for a friend
who was El Greco's brother, the one who used
to make love under the olive trees in Patmos
where the Apocalypse was written, a time when horses
ran free under the blessed eyes of John the Divine.

Two years later we met again
this time in Sibiu where you bought a painted horse
and I photographed you with a real one
outside the village museum, near a cross.
By that time I had become your warrior and sister,
painting horses only for you.
It was a green horse, remember?
In fact it was the grass in disguise,
it was the fish of the waterfall
swimming dangerously close to your heart.

The last horse I sent you
was ridden by an angel.
Its hooves made of diamond?
No, they were formed of the heaviest metal: tears.
This is why it keeps slipping
down the wall of your Sky House
sanctifying the path by which
the angel returns to the icon.

El Greco

Like a bird with clay wings
I threw myself
into your arms –
oh, the accordion swallowing
our old souls
with every note!

In his pocket the hanged man still carries
the rusty key of his lover.
Let us not cheat ourselves
even if this sea is overwhelming
and our bodies still young.
El Greco no longer has a body
yet how young he is!
Let us dedicate this poem to him,
this herd of galloping consonants.

Like a bird, I feather my wings
into the gift of the poem.

The Moon Seen from Romania, Japan and America

I try to penetrate this mystery: life or death?
while driving the highway, passing orchards,
speed limits, thinking of the old Buddhist nun near Kyoto
and my poet friend, a widow so young –
recreating our imagined three-way dialogue
between Romania, Japan, America – all within the same limits
of life, of death...

The answer comes when I least expect it,
a whisper scattered to the winds, tattooed
on the silken stem of a dandelion.
What are you two counting?
The unborn, already scattered petals of a hollow stem?
Here in Bucharest,
the bloom of each beginning seeds the sky and my mind
            with cruel questions
while insomnia takes the place of the moon against my night sky.

This comes as a letter to you, Tess.
I can see you near the Strait of Juan de Fuca
in your Sky House, alone with a cat on your lap,
faithful to your love-dream, a Cleopatra in blue jeans
trying to solve the same mystery: life or death?
and polishing with your own hair the white marbles,
the violet marbles, the infinite marbles of silence,
and the infinite stars of his absence.

I play again the tape you sent me, the one with
the Japanese writer, the nun shaping clay Buddhas
for the temple offering of love. Her voice, contralto
to your own, so patched with sighs and ellipses,
is accompanied by the rain of cherry blossoms against my window.
I can almost hear you pass the comb through your hair.

'Yes, yes,' you murmur as you listen to the nun's lament,
maybe half-truths about her dead lover.
It doesn't matter, together you launch fist-sized boats on the river
(a ritual for the dead) yours with a message for Ray,
and suddenly the pine trees shake their needles

into the river where he used to fish, as if to tell you
with those floating lancets that mark the current
how much he loved you –
and the nun's voice: 'Here in Kyoto we have the best moon,'
and your voice: 'I saw the moon last night and tried to take
a portrait of it, but my camera refused,'
and again your voice, like an echo whispering
on that Japanese mountain:
'I am thinking of making the title for my new book
of poems
    Moon Crossing Bridge –'

the mystery inside your conversation waxes
and wains while my speed accelerates
and I choose it: *life*.

Noroc

(instead of a letter, for Tess Gallagher)

'Noroc!' written by you on 'Weston Whisper Paper
25% cotton' – which reminds me of the cotton plantations,
and the hard work of the bodies and hearts in those times
– women working days and nights hoping for a sign of good luck
scrawled across America's too golden sky.
Only their children could live comfortably within a dream
which for them never came true.

Those women's eyes still search America's most promising sky.
From their cemeteries
they whisper into God's ear
tempting me, making me more daring,
more free.

Your drawing at the bottom of the page,
my portrait – maybe meant to do an angel's job
across the ocean, in a troubled Europe,
and, in the same heavily stamped envelope
I discover the photographs of your Japanese double,
your self-portrait stolen by a kamikaze
from an ancient art gallery
– in fact, an image you received in your sleep as a gift from Ray –

Your letter arrived on a hot day;
a bird struck herself against my window while I was reading it
and your pages suddenly turned into an arrow of good luck
directed towards my house here.

I liked even the mistakes made by your computer
such as: *creaved* instead of *craved*
          or
     liverty instead of *liberty*.
I invented a new meaning for them
such as: *crowned* for *creaved*
            and
     living in liberty for *liverty*.

90

Some would say: ordinary mechanical errors due to an explosion
in the sun
that scrambles words and feelings,
disseminating confusion.
But we know you wrote your letter before that cosmic event,
so these new words belong only to us
and I take them, not as mistakes of the cosmos,
but as Godsend.

Snapshot of an Orchard in Port Angeles
(for Mrs Georgia Bond and Stanley Kunitz)

The woman worked all her youth on Lost Mountain
marking trees to be cut,
and gave birth to five children.
Now, old and a widow, she takes care
of her orchard.
When her daughter brought the poet from Provincetown to visit,
the old woman was proud to show him
her oldest tree: *pinus aristata* – the one never marked
for cutting – that is, *the deathless one* – she added.

The poet doubted this: 'I'm afraid you're mistaken.
The oldest tree in the world is *metasequoia
glyptostroboides* – (also known as the Dawn Redwood)
and it has more lives to live. Well, what do you think?
Which of us is right, madam?'

She answered: 'A man lives as long as his life, mister,
but a poet lives as long as your tree with a strange name.'
He liked her answer so much that on her birthday
he sent by telegram to a nursery, then by truck
to her doorstep, his own tree, the Dawn Redwood,
and a card: 'May this tree grow near yours.
                Let their shadows annul each other reciprocally
                so in your orchard
                light will grow free forever.'

Golden Dust

In the golden dust of a September afternoon,
I try to entomb the ugliness of homely facts –
a bus with its cargo of gray hair,
the briefcases of bureaucrats, the heavy gold rings of butchers
striking against bone.
Yet beyond all, overwhelming everything,
the soft fragrance of the young insists on rising
like wild unripe strawberries.

NOTES

In the Forest *(page 23)*: Refers to Henri Rousseau's 'A Walk in the Forest' which is in the Kunsthaus Collection in Zürich.

Season's End *(page 25)*: Stanzas 2 and 3 refer to the lack of electricity and gas for heat and cooking during the Ceaucescu régime. It would come on only for short, unpredictable intervals, often in the middle of the night. Also during this period one would have to queue for several hours for bread and meat. The slogan 'we're for dialogue, not violence' was a post-revolution slogan, from the demonstrations in the University Square after the violence of the miners against students and intellectuals in Bucharest in that same space.

Rain in Sibiu *(page 27)*: The white flowers called 'Coins of Pity' in Romanian are called 'Honesty' in England. They can be dried and kept for years and are from the *Lunaria* family.

The Goldsmiths' Market *(page 36)*: The Goldsmiths' Market of the title refers to a famous old square in Sibiu, the *Piata aurarilor*, where writers and philosophers used to meet (see note for 'Dialogue').

Flowers of the Pyre *(page 37)*: In Romanian, the word meaning a funeral pyre – *rug* – is the same as the term for roses which is visible in the English term *rugosa roses*. The 'ancient town' of the last line is Sibiu.

With One Eye We Cry, with the Other We Laugh *(page 43)*: Avram Iancu: a historical leader who fought, in 1848, for the freedom of the Romanian people in Transylvania during the Austrian-Hungarian Empire.

Silent Voices *(pages 44-45)*: Cella Delavrancea was an eminent Romanian pianist, piano teacher, essayist, and memoirist, who, because she was a woman, only came to prominence in the very last years of her life. The poem alludes to a ceremony in honour of her work at the Romanian Writers' Union. The Romanian poet and novelist Gabriela Melinescu, author of 24 books, has lived in Sweden since 1975.

The Mirror's Hide and Seek *(page 46)*: The 'you' of the poem's beginning indicates the writer. In Romanian, the 'muse' who 'won't leave him alone' invokes death, the word for which, *moarte*, is feminine. *Mint:* for tea, for life, he's still the Priapus, god of the garden, in that world; mint is prolific, aromatic, giving.

Woman from Sibiel in Phoenix *(page 47)*: Sibiel is a village in the Carpathian Alps west of the city of Sibiu. In it is a famous museum of Romanian icons painted on glass.

Spanish Flashback *(page 49)*: The twelve grapes at the poem's close refer to one for each month of the year.

For Constantin Noica *(page 50)*: Noica was a great Romanian philosopher who deserves widespread acclaim. Translations of his writings have been undertaken by Liliana Ursu and Michael Naydan at Penn State College. Noica was born in 1909 and died in 1987. Under house arrest after the Communists took over, then 24-hour surveillance, he was imprisoned without trial, 1958-64. Upon his release he found his wife and children gone. Since he was banned from teaching, he then taught without remuneration, for the last 12 years of his life in Paltinis in the Carpathian mountains, living in great poverty. Students came to study with him on their own, and at some risk.

Really, Don't You Believe Me? *(page 51)*: 'We are the *number*' means 'We are the chosen'. The philosopher referred to is Constantin Noica.

Poem for a Brother in Spirit *(page 52)*: Ovid was the first poet exiled to Romania. He was sent in exile from Rome to Dacia which is the old name for Romania. He arrived in what was Tomis, but is nowadays Constantsa – a town on the Black Sea Coast. Tomis in Greek means amputation and 'what else could exile be other than amputation?' Liliana Ursu writes. Ovid died on the Black Sea Coast in Constantsa without ever being able to return to his beloved Rome and to his native town, Sulmona. Sarmizegetusa was the sacred capital of the Dacians where, defeated by Trajan in two wars, King Decebalus and his warriors committed suicide in 106 AD rather than surrender to the Romans.

Orpheus *(page 59)*: '*insieme, sempre insieme!*' means 'together, always together' in Italian. *Erebus*, in Greek mythology, is the embodiment of the dark, brother of the night, representative of the underworld.

Dialogue *(page 60)*: Goldsmiths' Market and Spine of the Dog Street are places in Sibiu. The Romanian-French philosopher, Emil (E.M.) Cioran, who has lived in Paris since 1937, was born near Sibiu in a village called Rasinari. As a student in Sibiu he lived on the street called 'Spine of the Dog', near the steps in the old section. The Goldsmiths' Market was where the city's craftsmen of gold jewellery once lived and worked. It has remained one of the most picturesque areas in Sibiu.

From the Angel's Window *(page 66)*: *Da capo* is a musical direction which means 'from the beginning' or 'over and over' – repeat.

Letter from the Constellation of the Swan *(page 73)*: Early Christians saw this constellation as the cross of Christ, Christi Crux. Today it is often called the Northern Cross or Cygnus. The Spring of Healing, or so-called Week of Illumination in orthodox Christianity, is an event commemorated always on the sixth day after Easter, a day when healing miracles take place due to the special sacred powers of holy water. It is represented by Virgin Mary because she is the one who gave birth to Jesus Christ, the Healer. In Romania, all places, especially churches or springs where miraculous healings took place, are called *The Spring of Healing*. It could be looked upon as a ritual of pagan Christian origins, since the Romanian ancestors, the Dacians, used to drink water from the Danube before they went to war so that if they perished they would become immortal.

Blues *(page 75)*: The *syrtaki* is a Greek line dance for men (forward, back a step, forward). It is fast paced, lively and uplifting.

The Eye of the Swan *(pages 78-80)*: In the second stanza, these are all books Liliana Ursu was reading in Pennsylvania on her Fulbright in 1992. The scene with the boulders in the fourth stanza is of stones barely visible under leaves outside the library window. Cismigiu is a park in Bucharest, the same one mentioned in Adam Sorkin's introductory notes.

The Moon Seen from Romania, Japan and America *(pages 88-89)*: The nun referred to is Jyakucho Setouchi, a well-known Japanese novelist, whose Buddhist temple near Kyoto is especially for women suffering from losses in love.

Noroc *(page 90)*: *Noroc* means good luck in Romanian.

Snapshot of an Orchard in Port Angeles *(page 92)*: Georgia Bond is the mother of the poet Tess Gallagher. Mrs Bond and the distinguished poet from Provincetown, Stanley Kunitz, are both avid gardeners on opposite coasts of America. The poem is based on Tess Gallagher's essay from *A Concert of Tenses*.